MY INFINITY

∞

MY INFINITY

poems

∞

DIDI JACKSON

Red Hen Press | Pasadena, CA

Book design by Mark E. Cull

Cover art: *Doves No. 2*, by Hilma af Klint, 1915, oil on canvas

Library of Congress Cataloging-in-Publication Data

Names: Jackson, Didi, 1970– author.
Title: My infinity: poems / Didi Jackson.
Description: First edition. | Pasadena, CA: Red Hen Press, 2024.
Identifiers: LCCN 2023054488 (print) | LCCN 2023054489 (ebook) | ISBN
  9781636281605 (trade paperback) | ISBN 9781636281612 (e-book)
Subjects: LCGFT: Poetry.
Classification: LCC PS3610.A3486 M9 2024 (print) | LCC PS3610.A3486
  (ebook) | DDC 811/.6—dc23/eng/20231201
LC record available at https://lccn.loc.gov/2023054488
LC ebook record available at https://lccn.loc.gov/2023054489

The National Endowment for the Arts, the Los Angeles County Arts Commission, the Ahmanson Foundation, the Dwight Stuart Youth Fund, the Max Factor Family Foundation, the Pasadena Tournament of Roses Foundation, the Pasadena Arts & Culture Commission and the City of Pasadena Cultural Affairs Division, the City of Los Angeles Department of Cultural Affairs, the Audrey & Sydney Irmas Charitable Foundation, the Meta & George Rosenberg Foundation, the Albert and Elaine Borchard Foundation, the Adams Family Foundation, Amazon Literary Partnership, the Sam Francis Foundation, and the Mara W. Breech Foundation partially support Red Hen Press.

First Edition
Published by Red Hen Press
www.redhen.org

MY INFINITY

poems

∞

DIDI JACKSON

Red Hen Press | Pasadena, CA

Book design by Mark E. Cull

Cover art: *Doves No. 2*, by Hilma af Klint, 1915, oil on canvas

Library of Congress Cataloging-in-Publication Data

Names: Jackson, Didi, 1970– author.
Title: My infinity: poems / Didi Jackson.
Description: First edition. | Pasadena, CA: Red Hen Press, 2024.
Identifiers: LCCN 2023054488 (print) | LCCN 2023054489 (ebook) | ISBN
   9781636281605 (trade paperback) | ISBN 9781636281612 (e-book)
Subjects: LCGFT: Poetry.
Classification: LCC PS3610.A3486 M9 2024 (print) | LCC PS3610.A3486
   (ebook) | DDC 811/.6—dc23/eng/20231201
LC record available at https://lccn.loc.gov/2023054488
LC ebook record available at https://lccn.loc.gov/2023054489

The National Endowment for the Arts, the Los Angeles County Arts Commission, the Ahmanson Foundation, the Dwight Stuart Youth Fund, the Max Factor Family Foundation, the Pasadena Tournament of Roses Foundation, the Pasadena Arts & Culture Commission and the City of Pasadena Cultural Affairs Division, the City of Los Angeles Department of Cultural Affairs, the Audrey & Sydney Irmas Charitable Foundation, the Meta & George Rosenberg Foundation, the Albert and Elaine Borchard Foundation, the Adams Family Foundation, Amazon Literary Partnership, the Sam Francis Foundation, and the Mara W. Breech Foundation partially support Red Hen Press.

First Edition
Published by Red Hen Press
www.redhen.org

ACKNOWLEDGMENTS

I am grateful to the editors of the following journals in which versions of these poems first appeared sometimes in different versions:

Academy of American Poets Poem-a-day: "Fall"; *Adroit*: "The Bell," "The First Bird"; *Alaska Quarterly*: "What You See is What You See" and "Witness"; *American Poetry Review*: "Aubade at Hawk Mountain" and "Void"; *The Atlantic*: "Poem with the Last Line as the First"; *Bomb*: "The Ten Largest"; *Florida Review*: "On Hawk Mountain, Vermont"; *Fugue*: "Early Morning Fires"; *Literary Matters*: "Considering Elaine de Kooning's Self Portrait #3," "The Fox," and "Spring Peepers"; *New England Review*: "The Burning Bush"; *New England Review Online*: Confluences: "Brancusi's Bird in Space"; *Plume*: "Medieval Notation" and "Mercy"; *Sewanee Review*: "The World as it Was"; *SWWIM*: "The Leisure of Snow"; *Virginia Quarterly Review*: "Awe"; *World Literature Today*: "Symptoms."

"The Burning Bush" also appeared in *Best American Poetry 2019*, edited by David Lehman and Major Jackson. *Best American Poetry* is published annually by Scribner.

"Ides of March, 2020" was anthologized in *Together in Sudden Strangeness: America's Poets Respond to the Pandemic*, edited by Alice Quinn.

"Considering Elaine de Kooning's Self Portrait #3" was printed in *The Ekphrastic Writer*.

Special thanks to SWIMM for the Residency at The Betsy in Miami Beach.

Once again, I want to give my most heartfelt thank you to Kate Gale, Mark Cull, Tobi Harper Petrie, Rebeccah Sanhueza, Monica Fernandez, and the whole team at Red Hen Press. I love you all and the books you work so hard to put out in the world. And a special thank you to Lisa Kruger, a fellow Red Hen poet, for believing in me right at the beginning.

Thank you to my colleagues at Vanderbilt University, especially fellow poets Kate Daniels, Mark Jarman, Rick Hilles, and Sandy Solomon, my friend and Chair Jen Fay, as well as friends and writers both here in Nashville and in Vermont. The Vermont Poetry Group saw many of these poems in earlier versions. Specifically, I want to thank Kerrin McCadden, whose wit and brilliance I adore as well as her own inspiring poetry, and who read the very first version of this collection. And my dear friend Michele Randall, whose support, endless hours of writing and revising, and twenty-five years of friendship are some of my greatest blessings. Also, I want to thank my friend Dana Nelson, who has been an example of strength and fortitude for me. I am so appreciative of your belief in me.

My gratitude also goes to my family. I am so deeply touched by the many ways you all have been there for me over the years. To my mother, Lois Gibbs-Joyce, thank you for your unconditional love and support. You inspire me. And to her husband, Bob Joyce. To my cousin, Nikki Schonert (who is really my sister), I want to thank you for all that you do to encourage me to be brave. I cherish our closeness, our late-night talks, and all the moments we've laughed until we've cried. Also, to my aunt and uncle, Shelia and Al Schonert, thank you for your belief in me. Also, thank you to our matriarch, Thelma (Tata) McCarthy, who passed away only months before the publication of this book. And to Amy and Jen and their families. And I want to express my immense gratitude for the fortune of sharing my life with Langston McCullough, Anastasia White, and Romie Jackson. You all bring me such joy. Having you as part of my family abundantly enriches my world.

Thank you to my Coven for your brilliance and your sisterhood. You all inspire me. Also, I want to mention how grateful I am for the guidance and emotional support from the weekly meetings with Matthew Dickman, Dorianne Laux, Michael McGriff, Joe Millar, and Sharon Olds. You are like family to me.

While this book was in the process of being written, I lost my dog Buzz of 16 years. He was my companion through the painful times and the joyful times. He moved from Florida to Vermont (where he fell in love with snow) and finally to Tennessee, where he only lived a month. But the emptiness of his loss has been filled by my feisty and spirited new little guy, Finn. He is my best companion in moments of both migraines and naps. But most especially, he is there when I write the really hard poems.

To my son, Dylan Berry, I am so proud of you. You are so strong, and I love to be witness to the responsible, courteous, diligent, and kind-hearted young man you are becoming. And to Lian Jacobs, you are such an inspiration. I am in awe of your drive, fortitude, and goodness. And I thank you both for making me laugh. The older I get, the more I need to laugh.

Finally, I want to thank my true guiding star, Major. I am blessed with your companionship, your wisdom, and your eternal love. Thank you for all you give to me.

for my mother Lois
&
for Nikki

CONTENTS

∞

∞

∞

CONTENTS

∞

∞

∞

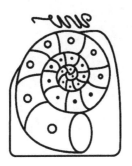

WITNESS

At this hour, on this day, in this place,
in this exact light, the birch leaves shimmy;
how they clap at the sun with their gilded hands
like images of early Christians in the ancient catacomb frescos
of Santa Pricilla, these trees too raise their open palms
to pray, then settle, bask in the late afternoon's golden glow.

The pair of ruffed grouse I flushed
earlier were frightened by only me,
two small firecrackers lifting
from goldenrod and milkweed, keeping low,
the earth too heavy for their want
of a higher flight. The Green Mountains
flex their muscles and like an old horse's withers
twitch a little with wind. They must know

summer is closing. It is their secret;
I am good with secrets.
A singular airplane scars the sky,
a metal bead lit like a speck of diamond,
heads straight for the crescent moon
still foggy in the twilight. I was never going
let myself be so small, but often I was
the only one to know the difference
between the ovenbird and the wood thrush,
between the time in college I wanted to be desired
and then deciding to do whatever a boy wanted
in order to get away. At twilight,
I'm the only one here to witness
the end of day, songs that quiet
the heat of the setting of the sun.

FALL

Do you know what I was, how I lived?
—Louise Glück

It is a goldfinch
one of the two

small girls,
both daughters

of a friend,
sees hit the window

and fall into the fern.
No one hears

the small thump but she,
the youngest, sees

the flash of gold
against the mica sky

as the limp feathered envelope
crumples into the green.

How many times
in a life will we witness

the very moment of death?
She wants a box

and a small towel
some kind of comfort

for this soft body
that barely fits

in her palm. Its head
rolling side to side,

neck broke, eyes still wet
and black as seed.

Her sister, now at her side,
wears a dress too thin

for the season,
white as the winter

only weeks away.
She wants me to help,

wants a miracle.
Whatever I say now

I know weighs more
than the late fall's

layered sky,
the jeweled leaves

of the maple and elm.
I know, too,

it is the darkest days
I've learned to praise—

the calendar packages up time,
the days shrink and fold away

until the new season.
We clothe, burn,

then bury our dead.
I know this;

they do not.
So we cover the bird,

story its flight,
imagine his beak

singing.
They pick the song

and sing it
over and over again.

AWE

We are the pattern makers . . .
　　　—Barry Lopez

What damage do I do?
The night avoids my eyes, so does the road.
I am never wholly myself, unto myself.

I have a friend who stops to bury
all the roadkill he comes across,
each journey he takes is like the end

of a war, the dead lining a road
that was supposed to lead to somewhere
greater. I saw the first firefly

of the season not out in the field
hovering like a star above the unwieldy
night grass, but on the window near the light

on my desk; his own light dark.
In these moments, I need to know
why the Luna moth has no mouth,

or if it was a sapsucker not a downy woodpecker
half decayed on the street near the elm.
For I too have held the dead in my bare hands,

my husband's body still marred
from what he had done
to himself. I wanted to wash each bloom,

each bruise, each yawning gash. Like my friend,
I want to leave nothing to strangers. I want
to bury all that I find with my hunger and awe.

BINGO CEMETERY, GREEN MOUNTAINS, VERMONT

A graveyard marks the trailhead
we take almost daily in all weather.
More often than not, on one of the graves
a bouquet of fresh flowers appears, chrysanthemums
I think, a stranger's morning prayers made manifest.
Some of these carved stones, large like granite ships,
are over a hundred years old. We move
up the trail as easy as rain. Once I fell
in love with the hills and crests of another
range of mountains. In those peaks I lost
my late husband's mind, soon to follow was his body
by his own hand. But this range can hold
buckets and buckets of snow, enough to freeze
the pain or at least keep it from thawing
without warning. Though on this day it is newly summer;
I stop to collect several recently dead
butterflies of the dozens that fill the air
like tickertape. The wings of the living opening
and collapsing like tiny breaths. And who can't breathe
in all this green? I take the dead home,
position them in a natural way, then pin their bodies
in a shadowbox, admire them even more if missing
a hind wing, a tattered or chipped forewing, some suffering
before the inevitable. I only collect those already dead
which means those that are imperfect. Each evening concludes
with the stained-glass sky. Maybe this place is church,
the forgiveness of sins, crucified relics of beauty,
a path that leads past and then toward the dead.

POEM WITH THE LAST LINE AS THE FIRST

In the end, I made myself live.
I am the farthest north of my life,

and I know I'm supposed to love
this world though I could shut the door

and pull the drapes until they overlap
like two palms in prayer.

But the tree lichens are shifting
from green to red and I miss the summer's scent

of lilacs and the bark pockets of trees
that fill with the nests of chickadees.

I understand the longing
for monastic life. All is slant

and when I read the Russian poets
I know I'm not the only one

who equates church bells with death tolls. Sometimes
the setting sun is too heavy for the mountains

to hold. How many times has your red hot
prayer slipped from your hands?

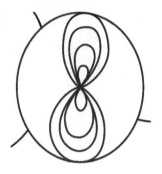

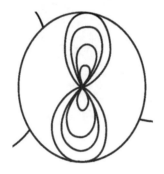

THE AUTOMATIC WRITING OF HILMA AF KLINT

> *It was not the case that I was to blindly obey the High Lords of the Mysteries*
> *but that I was to imagine that they were always standing by my side.*
> —Hilma af Klint

Hilma:

I wanted to see the invisible,
those interstates of light beams

that click easily into place
like the months on a calendar,

the imponderable lines that mark
then puncture a hole

into the next life, a place without
grass or dirt, without all that is

tangible in this world.
I learned the price

would be high to enter
the trance and talk

with those who were able
to drag themselves from bliss

toward all they might want
to forget. I pounded on the door

to unlock another reality.
Look at my hands as they scribble

the words decipherable only to me,
dictating in automatic text

the language of the dead,
like the alarm calls of birds

or the soft companion calls
they make to keep track of each other.

Look at my wrist spiraling
like a small snake sliding

from its skin, see as I catch
with each character all I need

to know with my pen. I'm another woman hungry
and ruthless for knowledge.

Listen to the four others
of De Fem warn me

of the dangers as they watch
my rhythmic and repetitive marks

fill notebook after notebook,
my sister dead over two decades

still a shadow on my wall
at night. Notice there is always room

at the séance for one
of the High Masters

to request yet another spiral,
another garden banded snail shell,

a continual growth,
the tail of the double helix

forming the exact ladder rungs
I will need to climb to finish my temple.

PRIMORDIAL CHAOS

after Hilma af Klint's Primordial Chaos, the WU/Rose Series,
Group 1, twenty-six paintings, 1906–1907, oil on canvas

Hilma:

Before Kandinsky, before Mondrian,
I dove into the pool
of the primaeval. Pigments of yellow
and blue became doorways into the oneness
at the origin of this giant world.
I was solo, my own bullet
twisting back to the tumultuous
beginning. No crystal words
strung and stored in my purse
like prayer beads, just the crowded
years of my life adding up to 44,
my age as I began this project,
a woman receiving grace
and direction through voices
from a different world instead
of bowing to tradition in my own. My jaw
lined with the light of abstraction,
convinced no one of my time
would want to look into the twenty-six windows
of the microscopic waters.
Even the nautilus, No. 5, is full
of dualities: hermaphroditic,
uniting the sexes, pulling the past
into the present, the horn of its shell
spinning like the helix of DNA,
like a metaphorical spiral staircase
that will lead the three of us, me, Wassily, and Piet,
to our deaths all in the same year,
1944—the war almost over,
Europe invaded and in flames,
everything a Big Bang.

EROS

after Hilma af Klint's Eros Series, The WU/Rose Series,
Group II, eight paintings, 1907, oil on canvas

Hilma:

On some, the patterns pulse like a flock of birds
    lifting all at once, their wings
        falling into the swing and figure

of their migration against a pastel background:
    the blush and roseate of spent phosphorous.
        On others, the ovals lapse like the humming future

surrounded by cryptic letters, the key known only to me
    and the High Masters who were preparing the way
        for a language of symbols that has

already existed forever. *The toolshed of my flesh*
    matches the peach toning of each canvas,
        a way for all the gears of color to be

prepped and supported. So modest
    and feminine, these eight canvases could almost
        be overlooked. But don't be deceived, they are

as mighty as the bombs their atom-like orbits could become.
    And though I will die one year before
        uranium destroys Hiroshima,

for me, Eros is the fusion of all colors. *For us*
    it is the opportunity to go blind
        or to wait for the asteroid

of the same name to pour past Earth
    once every 44 years in an oval orbit
        that blooms like a dazzling white aster.

DE FEM (THE FIVE)

after Hilma af Klint's The Ten Largest, Group IV, No. 7, Adulthood, 1907, tempera on paper mounted on canvas

Practice your drawings. They are pictures of drenching waves of ether which await you one day when your ears and eyes can apprehend a higher summons.
　　　—De Fem, received via psychograph, Feb. 21, 1905

I (en)

we were watching.
we watched so hard
　　　　　　we might have gone blind.
and we listened, too.
　　　　　　furiously we listened　　we began
　　　　　　to listen to the listening.
　　　　　　　　　　　　　　　　then the yellow bloomed
a beautiful atomic bomb,
a three-part Venn diagram,
the Trinity identified and dressed
　　　　　　　　　　in ballooning yellow blouses:

　　$u =$　　　*the spiritual forces of life*
　　$u =$　　　*everything in the world of spirit, truth, freedom, tranquility,*
　　　　　　　the reality of light, sacred desire, rebirth, woman

　　　　　　in the dusk　　we would call to each other's
　　　　　　disembodied voices　　we were girls
　　　　　　under a full moon　　the wolf moon of cold January

　　　　　　our breath a spirit just beyond our lips
　　　　　　like a lover we would one day take in
　　　　　　　　　　　　an inhale, a consuming.

　　$u =$　　　*the bond between the god within us and the soul*
　　$w =$　　　*to fight cunning and vanity*
　　$w =$　　　*everything that could be called a burden*

woman: as a girl I prayed to God
I would never get a period.

$w =$ *unease, life's material struggle and battle*

What are we without our bodies?

Woman.

II (två)

Listen to the shift
from rain to snow,
from wood to ash.
The change from pale grasses
to laced jewels,
from the dim pink sky
to something remembered.
Listen for the lift of robins
to spread their small fires
up and into the hackberry.

III (tre)

Happy with nothing
and with everything. Envious
of the dark coolness of the lake

in my childhood backyard, bed littered
with tightly closed paper pondshells
easily pried open with a small knife

which could split two cupped palms
ready to receive a spirit,
and reveal the flesh inside

and of course the pearly iridescent nacre,
the lake a backdrop for this violence,
this beauty. Primordial pond. Beyond

the cattails and duckweed, moccasins
thicker than leather belts nested, spawned
live-born babies, black lines of fear and death

and life, looped like cursive handwriting
as if they had been told what it was
I was listening for in my fistfuls

of day. This woman, a shadow moving
above the southern summer lake, digging
for something to devour.

FINITE

. . . and she skids out on her face into the light
                              —Galway Kinnell, *The Book of Nightmares*

I didn't notice how the sun
split and curled into small shavings

or how they each moved like snails,
slowly, of course, but also with waves

of muscle, contractions and pulses;
orgasmic. Nor did I notice

countless clutches of daylight
on my tile floor, right-handed coils

of ultraviolet and infrared light. I didn't note
the golden mean of shine, the nesting ratio

of radiant flux, the sun's mollusk revolution.
I wasn't able to see the day turn aperture,

turn curlicue, quirk and whorl, become the apex
of a shell, mother-of-pearl, iridescent.

THE TEN LARGEST

after Hilma af Klint's The Ten Largest,
Group IV, 1907, tempera on paper mounted on canvas

Childhood, No.2

Wasn't the blue just endless, the sky
I mean, that carried a band of jays
to the lake's edge, their clucks and whirs
curling back upon their bodies like infinity itself,
echoing off the water that sat as still as hammered steel
as the sun, like a head without a neck, spun
across the screen of sky—a giant orange
claiming its inheritance of the firmament.

To feel that escape, to run past the jasmine's
white pinwheels and follow the border of chain link
snaking its way to the water, careful
for moccasins and gators, my body a horn, electrified
with all that was wild, untamed. I tossed stones
the color of cinnamon and slate and watched the ripples
multiply, overlap like the hundreds of faces
I'd encounter as my future self. I risked
the savageness of the muck and cattails
for my father's rage inside the house. Always
a storm of words under our roof.
Once, on the day there was a solar eclipse,
a fox darted along the lake's shore, then up
into the neighbor's bed of roses. *She was*
the keeper of the kept secrets of the destroyed
stories the escaped dreams the sentences never caught
in words. She was my wild sibyl, my sister,
a piece of the fire inside of me that blew away.

Youth, No. 3

A spiral represents the ever-expanding universe. It is a symbol of growth, evolution, and expansion. The spiral is also a symbol of cycles and rhythm in nature.
—Chinmayi, Meditation and Ayurveda Coach

I escaped into the thicket of honeysuckle
that was now my body, a metallic taste
in my mouth once I started to bleed each month.
Like the sound of far-off thunder
when a storm fades and the sun re-emerges,
heating the late afternoon, all in technicolor,
glazed and sharpened with a crystal coat of rain.
Like keeping a spoon on the tongue too long
after the ice cream was gone. Still I retreated
to the lake where apple snail shells littered the shore
picked clean of meat by herons and coots.
Their spiraled eyes stared back at me
and the footprints I left near the cypress stumps.
Once they were a kind of currency, treasures
I could use to trade with the boys
in the neighborhood for matches
or trinkets precious only to kids.
This new physical body I inhabited
came to me overnight, my breasts no longer
flat nipples. I garnered the attention of men,
my uncle slipping his tongue inside my mouth
during a simple kiss goodbye.
                              That evening, the sky
was a deep orange, the only wavelength of light
able to travel so far at sunset: the blues and greens
scattering like dice. I wanted to spiral into myself.

Hundreds of snail shells lined my bookshelves
like a queue of mini universes,
each a humped cyclops bearing witness.
And even though it is an invasive plant,
I can't help but to love the honeysuckle,
to pull the string-like pistil through
the pinched base of the blossom
and suck the one bead of nectar. What a sweet dessert.
Each bush with hundreds of flowers all poised
with their own free drop of sugar.

Adulthood, No. 8, in conversation with Hilma af Klint's use of W

enter the darkest room in my house and speak
—Lucille Clifton

for G.B.

What if you never turn into winter?
What if the wreath is hung on the wrong door?

What if I let my mind go wooden, like a doll, and imagine
a woodcutter who removes all the memories?

His axe does such clean work.
He advises me to worship the blade

the moon makes when it wobbles like a scythe
in the night sky. Your wounds are all I think about,

those cuts along your wrists, the ones even worse at your neck.
I hear the whip-poor-will chant from outside my window

so I am sure to shut it each and every night.
It is a wonder I can still breathe with no air.

Everything is wrong. The song comes
in the afternoon rather than under the woeful moon

that sits in a woodpile of stars. Useless.
Oh how that day still howls. My grief

is an empty womb as pink as quartz.
You wove a blanket of wool that covers me,

the threads like worms. That wolf of a day,
the woodlands of my new grief:

you ate all the words, you fed me only worry.
Now it is all I can eat for years and years to come.

Old Age, No. 10

for M.J.

My Infinity. The pitch of yellow
on the rump of the warbler.
My palm flattened against yours
when we make love. My feral.
Your smile as wide as the sky.
The ocher blocks like bricks
that make a life. The grid
that stitches with black thread
all that holds together a day.
My lips that touch the tip
of that thread before it passes
through the eye of the needle.
Where the needle points.
How we follow the needle.
How I brake. How you add
more blue to your smile.
My empty envelope.
My imperfect. My curious.
Your drawer of silk and wool.
The flip of the number
eight to its side. The laying
down of infinity. How it is
almost invisible. How it is
in and around, under and inside,
everything. Your green.
Your continent. Your swing.
My twist. Our union.

THE TREE OF KNOWLEDGE

*after Hilma af Klint's The Tree of Knowledge, No. 2, The W Series, 1913,
watercolor, gouache, graphite, and ink on paper*

*You no doubt understand that is it necessary for the human soul
to be divided into two halves on the astral plane.*
—The High Masters via Hilma af Klint

The Vikings believed the boughs of an ash tree
could reach to the heavens, believed
its roots could thread hell.
This, the tree of helicopter seeds,
the tree that turns gold
or blood red in the fall like a martyr
dressed in the *shirt of flame,*
the tree destroyed by the emerald ash borer,
the tree that can change from male to female
as it ages. In No. 2, black and white swallows
spin on leaf edges and along the axis of the trunk.
They are as ancient as the tree itself
as ancient as the witch's knot at the base,
four points for the four elements:
earth, air, fire, water.
Above, the liquid songs, the incessant circling
all remind me of the swallows
in Greece where I spent the summer
after my husband took his life.
He was only 44. The same age as Hilma
as she started the paintings for the temple.
In Greece, I watched wings skim
the many eyes of icons
all rendered with their own suffering.
Now bearing witness to ours.
And whenever I bend over it is never
to smell something sweet like a rose or gardenia,
but rather to collect any yellowed
leaves. Surely they are a way to tally

the hundreds of hours he's been dead.
Even the swallows have a dawn song,
something they must wait on, count down to,
be prepared for when the moment is right.
Like Hilma, I want to decode it all,
but I'll never know why
I was left a widow.
Only that the two swallows are me,
dividing into two selves, my desire reawakening,
my sorrow forever rooted.

THE SWAN NO. 1

after Hilma af Klint's The Swan No. 1, The SUW Series, 1914, oil on canvas

They did not know that every hour every day, and not far away from there they were entering the legend of themselves.
    —Eavan Boland, *The Glass Factory in Cavan Town*

Hand in hand, De Fem call the dead,
bridge science and the occult.
Five women all like Eve looking for insight
into the sacred. Hilma, a medium,
her wind chime mind reaching the between,

her titular swans, a union of opposites,
the philosopher's stone—
a way toward the gold,
                —black swan / white swan
a horizon line of duality—

the end of a day spiraling
to the divine; her dead sister waiting
in the afterlife, and I know that space:
little beast heater growling in the corner
of my study reminds me that no one I love is

in Hell; they are near and far all at once.
These two swans' beaks press to one another
like old fruit, one's wings sooty branches,
the other's the riverbed under an early snow.
Both measure the span of a life,

a negative and positive of the other
except for the white swan's webbed feet, two blue
diamond eyes cutting the distance from the deceased,
both swans' own eyes closed, small seeds,
each monolithic neck a leaning obelisk.

MONSTER

Hilma:

I abandoned my desire for children, fed it to the monster
of ambition, that same beast whose song is sweet
yet who sits, saturnine, its mouth an ancient sickle
slashing at anyone who approaches wearing skirts,
blouses with billowed sleeves, collars like stiff pipes
around the neck, breasts tucked and carried as reminders
of birth status. Instead, I reckoned with the dead,
turned to a world where I held coins of credibility like gold.
My feet here on Earth, my mind a monsoon of colors
and symbols, a secret language entrusted to me
by the High Masters who lived beyond the grave.
Some called it lunacy, others genius. Blue was my color
for the feminine. Yellow the masculine. Green, oneness.
It couldn't be clearer to me and Anna as we took on roles:
Hilma: Asket for ascetic and Anna: Vestal, a priestess to tend the fire
of chastity. Oh dear. Oh dear *we would whisper to each other*
as the instructions from the other side spilled
onto the page and gobbled us up.

AFTER MY HUSBAND'S SUICIDE
I VISITED A PSYCHIC IN CASSADAGA, FLORIDA

and hoped for a way
    into the dark,

an escape hatch from this world
    toward his spirit, a handle

to pull that might open
    a trap door into eternity,

there the light would be as bright
    at the highest frequency

of my kettle's whistle,
    the sound like an arrow

landing miles away from the bow.
    That morning the psychic said

she wasn't herself,
    watched the oak near her door

shift into a red-tailed hawk, surely a sign,
    its voyage smooth across

the eye of her window as she prepared
    to speak with the dead.

She asked me to bring
    a piece of clothing, a coat

or shirt of the deceased,
    and a photo that she would slip

between the folds, tenderly,
        like lowering a coffin

into a grave. She mindlessly
        began to rub the cloth, her fingers running

its tucks and hems
        as if reading a braille text.

And that day I sat through my first and last visit,
        hoping to hear her utter

in a slightly southern accent the word *sugar,*
        his term of endearment,

something so sweet
        it could sting.

CHOICES

Hilma:

And don't you wish all the phosphorescence of life
could be handed to us in a paper envelope
or could be passed down handbook to leather handbook?
Favorite color of apron?
Hyacinth or daffodil? Beak or Feather?
Sometimes the prayer I whisper sags a little,
is missing the luster of a Medieval fountain
or the green shine of the spruce trees, their branches
spilling down a Swedish hillside.
                              Here's a thought:
hardly anything is known of the lives of women
artists. As if, like evening, they were all just temporary,
three-hour visitors, or, merely because of their presence,
made all else eventually blind.

I say we all become snakes, long and black.
We'll hide under leaf litter and in dark thickets,
our thin bodies will billow like ballooned cursive words.
Free from fear and historical.

THE BURNING BUSH

for Brianne Ortt (1979–2016)

An entire alphabet can be stuttered in a few gun shots.
So often it's the boyfriend spiraling down the chamber:
his words lodged in the barrel behind the bullet fast and frenzied.

We all wonder why the trash at the dump
never stops burning, why the blind look to the wind.
The rain stumbles outside the window:
the tombé before the heavy pas de bourrée of storm.

Cathedral de San Marco in Venice speaks
two languages: Greek and Latin, and I am jealous
of those with two tongues like the white pine
whose trunk cracks and whose needles whistle
to the bilingual nuthatch.

The sun torches the tips of the trees
on a descent from a world where no woman is safe.
Even the man who loved her wanted her dead.

The burning bush is an invasive species,
yet cardinals and chickadees flock to its red seeds
and flamed leaves in the fall. I should cut it to a stump
and rot its roots, but instead I admire its show of color,
watching the damage as it spreads.

SYMPTOMS

The day moon sits like a crooked smile
just above the horizon, spins
in a sky as blue as Mary's robe
and travels to Afghanistan
to buy lapis lazuli like the masters
of the Renaissance. It wishes it could inlay
the sky with bits of the lapis lazuli
and red coral like the Standard of Ur
and Sumerian art it admires. In fact,
the day moon is a master
of the twenty-first century. It lingers
near the chairs and coffee tables
of Eames and Nakashima. The day moon is jealous
of the lion's roar, wishes it could make thunder,
but only the clouds that hide the day moon
can make thunder. Sometimes
it feels so full it imagines exploding and releasing
hundreds of thousands of white moths
and everyone mistakes them for snow.
Other times, the day moon wants to vanish,
to see how thin and sharp it can become,
like a blade that hums with the whine of summer
mosquitos, and like the mosquitos
the day moon is out for blood.

EARLY SPRING

When I woke up, I was in a forest.
—Louise Glück

Maybe the forest floor's earliest flowers
are the signs you make yourself known to me,
make me human when I forget

I am: then and there begging for a sunrise,
or watching the woodcock's funneled flight,
or for the shy goldthread to feed

its own glossy leaves to the ruffed grouse.
I like small kindnesses.
I've waited a long time for the raw

to finally soften into something hungry
like the mouth that is
the grill of our car, embedded

in it a rose-breasted grosbeak,
limp, crushed like wrapping paper,
not yet hardened by death,

a kill I never wanted,
and because the ground was still
mostly the detritus of winter

his colors burned against the decay
as I dislodged his body
and placed it as if on an altar

under the not yet budded willow
hoping his flash of red might be mistaken
for red trillium, the same stench of death, the brilliance.

BRANCUSI'S BIRD IN SPACE

I move around the gold line
of a bird until I see a single feather,
the sky and song inside reflection,
an endless body balanced on beak,
the foot a hackle of bronze. I orbit
in and out of my wren mind
where my eye lingers not on the tip
but rather the center swell, the light
lean as if burdened to carry the weight
of another in the core belly of plume.
Death is rarely scheduled.

It may have been winter or maybe spring.
Did he drive my car or his? At seventeen
and already slightly swollen I entered a clinic
to clean up my life. Was I sure? Yes.
Even now, sometimes I'm sure the winter whir
of my ancient basement boiler is my molten past.
I wanted to consume all that made me
ache. No. I wanted to expel all that damned me.
I circle the bronze trying to find another way in
to its wing, to its powder down,
remembering the scrape and pluck.
I don't remember much

about Brancusi or the court case
affirming his cast metal as art.
Each night, the moon turns its same side
to the earth, forces tides to act
as brakes on our planet's rotation.
But I am spinning on brakes
worn out years ago.

MIGRAINE

Shard-glint of light on the sill,
run-on line of daybreak
at the hem of the front door,
incandescent orb in the bathroom,
torch of ice in the freezer—
these numberless galaxies
of light; all danger:
wasp sting
       gin burn
              gold plated bangles
too tightly wound around my wrist,
my eyes lined with black kohl
like the ancients. They will be volcanic rims,
right to left; top, bottom:
peacock's cry, cock's comb: a flamed flower,
edible, burning, reseeding, receding.
I'm sure there is a candle under the skin
on the right side of my face, its flame moves
from my jaw to cheekbone:
high cheekbones not flaming cheekbones:
zygomatic bone: yoke. When the war is over
I'll untie the knot of my brain.
I'll use tweezers like when I untangle gold
chains. My right arm is numb
except for my heartbeat: fleshy
and heavy. Where is the darkness in this day?
All the light will be smaller tomorrow:
in this way, I feel closer to the dead.

EARLY MORNING FIRES

for Anya Silver who died too soon (1968–2018)

I've never known days this long,
mornings strung like crystal prayer beads,
clacking day into day. I am clumsy
at daybreak against the glassy mountains
and flocks of fog. I walk gingerly
down the steps to sunrise, open a window,
disturb a spider the size of my thumb
whose web, thick and cottony, holds parts of wings
and moth antennae tucked like Egyptian amulets
into the mummy's linen shroud.
So much of living is about death.
I learned of yours just last night
while cooking dinner, a simple joy
suddenly pitched with the pain of losing you.
In August everything grows so hard
and so fast. I too catch the frenzy to live.
This morning, the hydrangeas sag
like white waxen death masks.
Like me they know the end
of summer is close.

THE FOX

One red fox crosses Route 100
skittering past our front tires—
a few yards up, another.

We could be near or half a world from
our home. Wheeling
in our seats, we try to catch

a glimpse of these two fiery hymns,
their chanting footsteps
crossing the familiar spine of a road.

I bless your ears and eyes,
and remember last winter when we watched
a fox span a snowy field, pause,

then call the other, as if with small bits of thunder,
and it was then I asked myself
how shall I live?

The dead have no lovers
and I was young and dead
until you swerved enough.

Four young birch trees
penciling the road sag knowing
that everything almost dies and then does.

For what are our eyes?
For what are our ears?
Into whose mouth are we followed?

That night we are kept awake by the moon
following the mountains' ridge
like the tracery of a child.

In the morning, all the lines are erased.
We have coffee, read the news,
and see shards of red flashing across our screens.

MEDIEVAL NOTATION

On the first half of our hike the snow
was at our backs, on the second—the return,

it pelted our faces as we watched
spring instantly cloak itself

becoming monkish for another
several weeks, the wind a Gregorian chant,

the deer prints crossing our path
a square notation, maybe medieval.

All of this despite the spiders
who, back at the house, like small multi-armed gods

move easily across the heavens of our ceiling.
Even a moth gripped our window screen

just two days ago. Two days too early.
The world's rhythm is set

with or without us. And I was pregnant
and then I wasn't, and who

could blame me for wanting the world
to spin past me just that once.

We know the green below
the new layers of snow

will eventually become all there is
to see. Perkins Brook leads to Bingo cemetery,

the spot where we always start our hike.
It is our beginning. It is a beginning.

LATE DECEMBER

A new year arrives, distant like my fingertips

backlit by a flashlight, like a robin's

twilight canticle, like the few feathers

from a kill discarded at the base

of the laurel, like notes of a bosc pear

rotting in the bowl, like the stray dog's quiver,

like a rare slice of steak, like the dried

hydrangea from the memorial, like the paper

wasp's perfect geometric guild, like the image

I reflect back to God, like an infection

of distemper and Lyme, like the thread-thin

bones in the wild caught salmon,

like the crunch of those bones in my mouth,

like the last tiny white stone placed atop the cairn

at the edge of the field, like that stone

falling the next day, like picking that stone

up and placing it on the top of the stack again.

THE LEISURE OF SNOW

With the leisure of the snow
falling like a Rothko

over the morning, I am astonished.
Although chickadee and titmouse flurry

to the feeder, they do so as timid as winter light
which daily asks for a little more patience

in order to emerge from the frigid night.
The flakes tumble as slow as prophecy,

occasionally buoyant on an invisible breath.
I do not suffer insomnia. I prefer to beat

the dawn; but this I shouldn't have to explain:
for the morning is naked and beautiful

and yawns many times before turning
on the light. I am there

to see. The birds drop in and out
like lures in a dark ocean littered

with loitering stars. What a drowsy way
to start the day with the silence of God.

TATTOO

for Susan Rothenberg

How do I crack open the blue? I mean
like a horse running through a canvas
straight toward me, all four legs suspended
like Cyrillic, like a tattoo, like
humanity, a vibrating mass of bronco, agitated
surface of skin and mane, blue like another day,
ghostly outlines of a hieroglyph, lapis lazuli,
a prehistoric line of ankle and hoof, the desert
with limitless sky, a flash of angled withers, a clapper
with no bell. Wait, you were the bell.

May 20, 2020

THE FIRST BIRD

The first bird I see in the brand-new year
is a chickadee, and according to birders
it is now my theme bird, industrious, curious,
no jukebox of melody but instead a 2 or 3 note
simple song, the dropped tones of *hey sweetie*
outside our bedroom window where we rest
a moment, naked, our desire rooting us to each other,
our ankles like anchors, your coined eyes
on my Willendorf figure, my freckles
like splashes of sweet vermouth. It is winter and the heat
of the room tricks us into cracking a window
to allow the smallest ribbon of yellow to touch
the bed, then to move across your face
like a honeyed blessing of mercy. I know the days
of the calendar itch like fledglings, each at the lip
of their nest, ready for flight; and that your parents
told you not to wish your life away,
but how esoteric of them, the old, though now
we are the age they were. Lip to lip. Nose to nose.
Belly to belly. And on this cold day, I want
to eat you. An excoriation of your body
in the manner of the eucharist.
For if you become part of me,
then I will know and help carry all
of your suffering, and you mine.

"WHAT YOU SEE IS WHAT YOU SEE"

Frank Stella would be proud of my migraines
especially those that come after sex—

exquisite pleasure, then blindness,
the hard-edged jagged lines with Day-Glo colors

that grow into a barbed crescent
eating at one side of my head until it passes

like a lit-up road sign: paracentral,
mid peripheral, far peripheral—gone.

Then the veery picks up the flute
outside my window and I can hear

every tiny whirl inside the metal pipe
of its throat, a song some in the 19th century

called seductive, and finally I can find
my clothes and smell the ground coffee we made

hours ago, sheets pungent with sweat,
the rain a few miles away. Under this geometric spell

and pills like wasps beneath my tongue,
I am the closest to my true self,

and I secretly love my agony
just as I love the blue webbing of veins

on my legs, wrinkles like tidal ripples
on my face. I know that the pain will come

and eventually go. The birches grow still
before the storm, like they want to hear us,

like they are voyeurs listening in
to both kinds of my ecstasy.

AUBADE ON HAWK MOUNTAIN

This is the time of year we sleep
with the windows open
even in the rain,
hoping the sill and floor stay dry
enough. Birdsong begins
before the sun
with what sounds like
a thousand voices, flitting thresholds
of consciousness in the trees.
Yesterday we saw a garter snake
sunning itself on the trail to Sunset Ledge,
and a dozen red trillium lined up
to salute the eastern sun, their petals
already pungent and corpsey for carrion flies,
what gossip they can tell of winter,
bulbs inches deep, nestled together
for months and months.
Still under the down, we are nude
and touch each other's bodies
in the pre-morning light. Rain checks
our breathing and it is here I tell you
of my dream of collecting yolk after yolk,
so many a large bowl fills
with a hundred tinseled suns.
But we don't see the sun
anytime soon, we exhaust ourselves
and return to sleep as the morning slips by
on young and impatient feet.

ON HAWK MOUNTAIN, VERMONT

I am parting with the sun
that like a Greek oracle
descends the temple of mountains
before me. Their silhouette
darkens to Oxford blue,
elides the current of the sky
until I no longer see
crest or peak. After moving up
from the South, how much should I know
of coniferous trees or of chickadees
who play their winter song of *fee bee, fee bee,*
the last note toppling an octave from the first
like a softly closing door.

The Northern sky stands so straight,
it uses the largest pines for crutches;
they bend under its weight.

We have a friend who isn't happy
I'm white. With him, though, the road
is sampling the sound of the rain.
My husband and I hold hands
as often as we can,
each finger erupting a new continent.

But in the early evening,
I worry that if pulled over,
when my husband lifts his empty hands
he is lifting only his blackness.
At this hour a chickadee cries
in staccato: *dee dee dee, dee dee dee.*
I wonder how it knows my name
before I look at our marriage
in the milky evening light.

VOID

After three weeks of being left in the house
to dry and set, the two Eastern tiger swallowtails

I collected from the road,
already dead and broken into small pieces

like the painted parts of mechanical toys,
were mysteriously eaten, all save the wings.

And of course, I love the wings most:
the sooty tusk-like stripes pouring

from the arched top wing, its velvety black border,
and thorax gone like Hepworth's oval void.

It is the year of the hole says Henry Moore
in 1932. I am afraid it still is.

I mean, the year of the hole. I mean
1932. My husband, for our anniversary

bought a Celestron Skymaster 25 x 100 in order
to scan the stars and all the blackness

that surrounds them. I watch him
watch the heavens. He decides which are planets,

which are satellites, which are fodder
for black holes. But it is too simple to know

where all the emptiness resides,
how these gaps can give way

to something hungry, or worse yet,
something that steals all of the light.

MARE CRISIUM

from Rochester, Vermont

> *Do I really want to be integrated into a burning house?*
> —James Baldwin, *The Fire Next Time*

The nights I dread are the ones
my husband craves the surly half-self
of the pocked moon, the nights he steps into the darkness
of our porch, up to the barrel breath
of the indirect light, wants the clouds to clear,
wants to photograph the Sea of Serenity.
I ask him about the Sea of Crises—
a new name for the earth?
Torch-wielding whites march at state capitals
as homes in St. Helena are consumed by the Glass Fire.
But the understory of open sky
dismisses my seriousness as if
all will remain as is:
                            in such grand emptiness
I cling to the familiar: the nightlight
I click off, the serpent-smooth metal
of the tripod. The moon's marias emerge
like age spots, monochromatic & ashy;
a congregation of trees encircles the small grip we have
as a barred owl heckles a question.
Everything at my age comes as a warning;
I have no knowledge or truth, have only
the premonition of my pallid skin catching fire
with each click of my husband's camera.

HOW TO WRITE A LOVE POEM

Join the chorus in the rustling cedars,
the small chirrups in the night
of fuss and feather, and wonder
on the exact time the moon might rise fully
in order to compete with the street lamp,
its face flecked with snow, its neck a swan
dipping into the earthly dark.
And be sure to attend to the alphabetical sheets,
and allow their twisted story to be told.
Don't hesitate to doubt their stillness.
And never count the twelve stairs
to the second-floor bedroom
or the silver buds on the magnolia
just beyond the back door, waxen
and sealed for winter. Instead
consider the Northumbrian coast
and the train along its spine.
Alnmouth to Edinburgh. Leave time for tea.
Be sure to note how gray
the ocean might be, as your tongue
tucks into the roof of your mouth
like a small animal in the silence
and vastness of the day.

after Traci Brimhall

VIGIL

I'm learning to tend fire,
watch the day go blind
and take small steps
on ice that feels like teeth
grinding against pavement.
I'm learning to leave
the spiders to their webs
like the one in the corner
where the bathtub meets the floor.
I also leave the husks of flies
to dangle there like chimes
for fear of breaking the silk.
I'm learning to look
to see if the moon will rise
or set over Hawk Mountain.
It often surprises me,
although some nights
I can't see it at all.
I understand now
that chickadees, like patient tourists,
take turns at the feeder
and will not for any amount
of sunflower seeds
crowd the bird before.
I just learned how to correctly cut
a pomegranate in a way
that won't look like a blood bath
in my kitchen. I am learning
that the call of the barred owl
sometimes sounds like our neighbors
laughing outside in the dead of winter.
I realize maybe it *is* our neighbors

in their hot tub and not an owl at all.
During a snowstorm,
I've figured out how to flip
my windshield wipers up
like raised antenna,
my car a frozen moth.
I've learned how to keep
ashes in the firebox that heap
as high as decades.
They remind me of
his ashes, the ones
I kept on my nightstand.
They help the coals
catch fire in blue mornings.
And I know now how
to look for signs,
those pagan symbols
on tree bark and in bird song.
Though I'm always looking
for the answers
I'm not sure I'll ever find.

TWO-HEADED WOMAN

for Lucille Clifton

There are so many days we want to speak
   to the dead. No one really waits for the fall

festival of Samhain to acknowledge
   the secret bodies that like white asters

bloom all around us. Many of us know
   and are unafraid of the thousands of bonfires

of souls still curious about the frills of life.
   Even Lucille couldn't ignore

the ancient calling to place the planchette
   down over the letter G on the wooden Ouija board,

the spot to begin the separation of skepticism and belief.
   She learned of the things we all know now

as the heart glided letter to letter, a little flame
   at its center to remind her of the inevitable winter

to come. And at that moment, I imagine the wind
   picking up, a spoon or two

dropping from the counter in another room,
   someone shouting fire as the twigs in the ash pit

spark and spit, her face hot not from the flames
   but from all she learns, that knowledge

like a pearly white tooth
   gnawing at her from the inside out.

NECROMANCY

And then the room stilled. Just outside the window
the robin took flight, the elm's thin arms thrashed
against the glass, and we settled in,

our fingers touching the edges
of the planchette, a heart adrift
on a sea of letters: talking board, spirit board,

witch board. Words came as if on radio waves
carried by the wind. The blackness of the unknown
was a giant pond into which we were willing only to go

ankle deep. We covered mirrors so the deceased
would not be trapped, so whoever answered
our auction-like calls and queries could return

to where they came from. No one wanted
to play medium. Our dimmed lights flickered
like tiny asterisks. I was lost in the thicket

of my dead. We all have too many.
My friend watched two husbands
slowly die of cancer. Twice a widow,

her strength melted like sugared candy
under her tongue. So many questions
we all have, tucked under our living-being wings.

Us, small baby birds quaking at the edge of a nest,
testing our feathers for flight.

CHOCOLATE

Sholeh sent me a video
      on how to make chocolate with cardamom,

cayenne, carraway seeds, even blood
      oranges with the rinds still wheeled in place.

The stars are hiding behind the city lights
      where I find myself exactly one month from summer

though black flies swarm my husband's head
      like exhaust and know only these warm, wet days.

I argue the meaning of everything
      that is manmade. We left seed

for the feeders inside the house while away,
      long enough for a mouse to chew an entire room

into the bag and die there, its body still a bit soft,
      so new in death there was no smell, just the fur

like a pile of ash, like Debussy's compassion for flute,
      spare as if in a field somewhere. I couldn't bear

the body so I tossed it under the cedars
      to be eaten by that which eats the dead.

None of the stars lie, so I leave my window open
      late into the night to listen for their shrinking

while the chocolate cools and hardens for us
      to break into pieces and eat with tea tomorrow.

IDES OF MARCH, 2020

Two doves land in the moss
below the feeder,
sunbathe in the last light
of an early spring day then huddle
on the lower branch of the ancient
hackberry tree where we wait to see
them mate. By today,
the newest plague has killed
thousands in Italy,
so any life is good life.
The 2016 Viberti Dolba
although not communion
feels sacred—
as do our crackers and cheese,
our hike under a biblically blue sky,
our fire raging in its cage
when we return home.
I have complained about so much
for so often, how now do I love
that tiny fellow chipmunk who
on hind legs checks the celestial movement
of the sun before digging what I imagine
are Christian catacombs under our foundation?
He has a mission. So should I.
No rain today fell into the open
graves of the dead, only a sunset
and life as we know it.

FORECASTING

poem with the first line by Lucille Clifton

Oh, *to be the mad woman at the river's edge.* To gnash my teeth,
to paint my face gold like the evening sky. To kneel

when the loons begin to call, haunting and full of weather.
On nights when the wind uses the bare spring branches

like whips, when its gusts are so grand I'm sure
there will be dents in the dusky sky,

I know the dead near. Not because
of the way broken sticks land under the stormy elm,

their pattern foretelling misfortune or emergency.
And not because of the flecks of tea

at the bottom of my cup spiraling into love loss
as I sit safely inside my house.

Nor because of the way the stacked whorls
of my fingerprints remember the kerosene, the knife tip.

But because if I had a well, I would lift from the dark
the brown bucket of your body. You would be filled

with spring water, pure as a new year. The wheel of the pully
a giant eye, a spinning witness to all that went wrong.

MIGRAINE

I have the tunnel vision of a Cyclops
as the wreckage of the day shatters
into murderous cracks and angles,
vibrating metal shards, chromatic devils
from beyond. I go wild-eyed, bound now
to the pain that will wash over me,
my medicine a far-off rope for rescue and release.
How could I have survived these episodes
a hundred years ago or more?
Surely a symptom of a woman's weak mind,
evil spirits to be released by a drilled hole
into the skull, and for extra measure,
garlic to plug the cavity in case of witchcraft.
I would be considered hysterical, too delicate,
using my pain to avoid the female role
of sex as duty to my husband. A low benchmark indeed.
But what vivid hallucinations I am treated to
for a few moments at least. A spectacle
of blooms, a parade of geometry, a coating
of mutated botanicals.

AIRS

The yellow tulips are rangy.
The yellow tulips are mouths

of sunlight. You sit
at sunrise and curl

like a leaf, brown and little.
Sometimes you leave

your shoes on in the house,
in the bedroom. Sometimes

you rub your hands against the old
popcorn ceiling as if reading braille.

Where is the good luck? The pot of gold?
The yellow tulips are tiny priests.

On Tuesday you sit
at the edge of the world like an icon

ready to bless all of humanity
with two limp fingers.

The gray stone fireplace pops
out a hymn. The gray stone fireplace knows

when to stop humming.
The yellow tulips only know flattery.

The yellow tulips will die
of vanity.

SPRING PEEPERS

I try to record their song
lifting from the pines and birches,

one solitary note—*shrill*—then three
—*trill, trill*—then twelve or twenty,

all at once like a reunion of women
at a kitchen table: my aunts and grandmothers

with wine in hand & cigarettes bouncing
to the syllables of the names in their stories,

their ash-flick of grief.
Why is dusk so melancholy?

A vesper of tree frogs begins
with or without me. I often sit

and watch the end of the day
turn to a steely gray. Those women

each claim their widowhood. Like the X
on the back of the peeper,

we are all marked
one way or another;

maybe we carry the sign from birth,
maybe from generations before?

Each woman in my family
has buried a husband;

in that line I am the last.
Bits of night begin to unravel,

as the song swells
and slowly covers the sky.

THE WORLD AS IT WAS

When the moon has gone I fly on alone
                    —W.S. Merwin

That wolf of a day, the woodlands of my new grief:
you ate all the words, you fed me only worry.
Now it is all I can eat for years and years to come.
You wove a blanket of wool that covers me, the threads
like worms. My grief is an empty womb as pink as quartz.
Everything is wrong. Even the whip-poor-will calls
in the afternoon rather than under the woeful moon
that now sits in a woodpile of stars. Useless.
Oh how that day still howls. I hear it call
from outside my windows so I am sure to shut them all
each and every night. It is a wonder I can still breathe
with no air. Your wounds are all I think about,
those cuts along your wrists, the ones even worse at your neck.
I let my mind turn wooden, like a doll, imagine a woodcutter
who can remove such memories. I hope it is his axe
that would do such clean work. He advises me to worship
the blade the moon makes when it wobbles like a scythe
in the night sky. What if I just woke up and the world
was as it was? What if you never turned into winter?
What if the wreath was hung on the wrong door?

THISTLES

There's a cotton dress in my closet
that reminds me of the thistles

that fill the fields of Vermont's Taconic Ramble,
stack like stars and grow as tall as a decade,

their purple flowers like promises
of something kind, something as sweet

as river-song or as soft as the tiny scales
on moth wings that we all mistake for dust.

It is in July I think of purple
and cotton clothes, crescent paths

that cut through acres of green, the mountains
waiting the arrival of everything that sings

and turns glam despite the cruel. And it was
this spot I visited many times

on the anniversary of your death,
once, despite the quiet of the hills

bundled like boxes under the tender sky
I suffered a migraine, my vision shattered

into an abstract pageant of pain, a prism
of colors as sharp as any knife.

AFTER THE SUICIDE

Near the end of the day
the chickadees never hesitate to scold

my entrance from the trail into Flanders Field.
I take their flush and feather,

tick them off with the last shards of sun
and the skeletal underside of a cloudless sky.

The mountains begin to silhouette not knowing the names
of the dead profiles they resemble. I am

hypnotized by the sunlight. It is dusk
that changes what I think I see

into what is. And when I read the word *lost*
I read *Lota*, Bishop's partner

who like my own husband took her life. And there
I go, once again nailed by the starving sky and the tack-sharp pines

to this story despite the day dying;
despite wanting to forget the dead

and instead dwell on what I might offer the world,
despite turning from the recently mowed meadow

of milkweed and curled dock, the empty crabapple trees
and their black scowling boughs,

to head back down the path, book in my arms,
swallowing a scream clanging like a bell in my throat.

HALO

When the forecast calls for frantic, fiasco.
When the forecast calls for saints and slugs.
When the forecast calls for Sexton and Plath.
I know someone has left this earth.
When the prophecy is hail followed by tornado.
When the prophecy is ripple, wing.
When the prophecy is another prophecy.
I drop to my knees and touch my skull
to the loaf round belly of my dog and weep.
When the prognosis is necrosol, granite.
When the prognosis is telephone, elegy.
When the prognosis is egg, caterpillar, butterfly, sky.
When the prognosis is scripture, scripture, scripture.
When the mechanism is knife and heart and blood.
When the mechanism is two waxwings, cherry tree.
When the hair. When the teeth. When the nails are compost.
When you are halo. You are halo.

MERCY

I prefer the charred smell of old fire rings,
tattooed evidence of laughter
like the kingfisher's rattle at the water's edge,
the shoreline the pallor of my skin; who am I
to be witness to the infinite
number of jays winging down the mountain—
blue beads weaving in and out of pine and beech
jeweled and brilliant? *The air itself is their memory.*
There is no freedom like that. The mountains
are multiple continents. How do I pray
to anything larger than this? Everything
is of me and so much greater
than me. And why quit this place?
Birch branches softly drum my name.
And when I say quit, I mean intentionally,
as with blades or guns, pills even.
Miracles fall everywhere like loose leaves.
A ghost rests in my arms and I rock him
for a moment as he remembers what was
good: the cool nights, the warmth of campfires,
the mercy that strips us naked to each other.

Notes

"Awe" is dedicated to the Chip Blake.

"The Automatic Writing of Hilma af Klint" is written in the voice of Hilma af Klint as are many of the poems that follow. They are completely imagined thoughts and conversations.

The Swedish artist Hilma af Klint (1862–1944) painted what we now realize arguably to be the earliest examples of abstract art, predating Kandinsky and Mondrian. At 44 years old, she began the cycle of work titled *The Paintings for the Temple*. The "temple" did not yet exist. She was called to create these paintings after contacting guides from the spirit world through her practice of spiritualism. She, along with four other women, formed De Fem. They met regularly and communed with beings of higher consciousness beyond the grave by conducting seances, using psychographs, and creating automatic writings. But it was af Klint who was selected to single-handedly create the required paintings for the temple (193 in total) between the years 1906 and 1915. She completed these painting in two parts. Part I (1906–1908) and Part II (1912–1915).

"Primordial Chaos" is the first series af Klint completed for *The Paintings for the Temple*. Group I. (November 7, 1906–March 15, 1907).

"Eros" is the second series af Klint completed for *The Paintings for the Temple*. Group II. (January 18–September 30, 1907). Wassily Kandinsky, Piet Mondrian, and Hilma af Klint all died in 1944. She was 44 when she started this large cycle of paintings, and the comet, Eros, passes the earth only once every 44 years. The lines "preparing the way for a language of symbols that has already existed forever" and "Eros is the fusion of all color" are direct quotes by Hilma af Klint from her journals.

"De Fem (The Five)" is responding to *The Ten Largest, Group IV, No. 7, Adulthood*, 1907. Section one invokes the imagined voices, as if in a Greek Chorus, of De Fem, the five women af Klint met with regularly and who all attempted to reach and communicate with the High Masters. The symbols and their translations come from af Klint's notebooks. The symbols *w* and *u* had multiple though similar meanings to af Klint and were used extensively in her paintings. The notebooks she kept were complex though thorough and serve as a window into the meaning of her otherwise enigmatic work.

"The Ten Largest" is the most well-known of af Klint's series for *The Paintings for the Temple*. Group IV. (October 2–December 7, 1907). The italicized lines in "Childhood, No. 2" are from W.S. Merwin's poem, "Vixen."

"Tree of Knowledge" Hilma af Klint painted this series in two versions with seven paintings in each version. Both are in Part II, paintings from 1912–1915.

"The Swan" Hilma af Klint started "The Swan" series just after the beginning of World War I. She began them in September of 1914 and turned 52 in October. Sweden remained neutral. However, these are considered some of her darkest work. Each painting in the series becomes more and more stylized until the swans all but disappear into geometric cubes and concentric circles. This series explores her interest in dualism.

"Monster" Anna in this poem is Anna Cassel, the first woman to work with af Klint and later help her to form De Fem.

"Burning Bush" is dedicated to Brianne Ortt, my former dance student who was killed by her estranged boyfriend in a murder-suicide.

"Brancusi's Bird in Space" Constantine Brancusi was stopped by customs agents questioning if his bronze sculpture, "Bird in Space," was actually art as he claimed. If it was a hunk of metal, as they suspected, they could tax it. A court case ensued.

"What You See is What You See" is a quote from Frank Stella.

"Two-headed Woman" is an African term used to describe a woman with the ability to speak to spirits in the afterlife. It is also the title of a collection of poems by Lucille Clifton.

BIOGRAPHICAL NOTE

Photographer: Sarah White

Didi Jackson is the author of *Moon Jar* (Red Hen Press, 2020). Her poems have appeared in the *American Poetry Review, Alaska Quarterly Review,* the *Kenyon Review,* the *New Yorker, Oxford American, Ploughshares,* and *Virginia Quarterly Review,* among other journals and magazines. She has had poems selected for *The Best American Poetry,* Academy of American Poets' Poem-a-Day, *The Slowdown* with Tracy K. Smith, and *Together in a Sudden Strangeness: America's Poets Respond to the Pandemic.* She is the recipient of the Robert H. Winner Memorial Award from the Poetry Society of America and was a finalist for the Meringoff Prize in Poetry.

www.ingramcontent.com/pod-product-compliance
Lightning Source LLC
Jackson TN
JSHW081501070125
76711JS00004B/68